Unusual Latin America (and Antarctica)
Traveling on the Edge

Alan M. Davis

Library of Congress Cataloging-in-Publication Data

Davis, Alan M. (Alan Mark)
Unusual Latin America (and Antarctica) / Alan M. Davis

Includes index
ISBN 978-0-9960283-7-0 (paperback)
ISBN 978-0-9960283-8-7 (e-book)
1. Travel. 2. Latin America. 3. Antarctica.

Copyright © 2017 Alan M. Davis All Rights Reserved

Photograph credits:
All photographs © 2017 Alan M. Davis except for the following: Mini Cooper, page 8, © 2017 Pinterest, www.pinterest.com/pin/459930180669819180; custard-leaves-tree-thailand-1549276, page 50, © 2006, pixabay.com; harpy eagle, page 50, © 2012 Michael Z. Davis; Casarões em estilo colonial no Largo do Pelourinho, Centro Histórico de Salvador, page 68, © 2009 Adenilson Nunes/SECOM and Turismo Bahia; Capoeira on the streets of Sao Paulo, page 68, © 2016 Marius Becker, sports.vice.com.

No part of this book may be reproduced in any written, electronic, recording, photocopying, or other means without written permission of the publisher or author. The exception is in cases of brief quotations embodied in critical articles and reviews.

Although every precaution has been taken to verify the accuracy of the information contained herein, the author and publisher assume no responsibility for any errors or omissions. No liability is assumed for damages that may result from the use of information contained within.

Publisher: Scrub Oak Press
               9975 Wadsworth Pkwy #K2-118
               Westminster, CO 80021-6814

10 9 8 7 6 5 4 3 2 1

Table of Contents

Preface iii

About the Author iv

Chapter I. Getting Shot in Bogotá 1

Chapter II. Car Manufacturing in Uruguay 7

Chapter III. Two Hidden Gems of the Caribbean 13

Chapter IV. Broken Gem of the Caribbean 17

Chapter V. The Cuban View of Cuba 21

Chapter VI. The Amazon Headwaters, Ecuador 25

Chapter VII. Searching for Jaguars in Bolivia 29

Chapter VIII. Plantation Owners of Suriname 35

Chapter IX. Iguazú 41

Chapter X. Meeting a Monkey-Muncher 47

Chapter XI. Drake Passage and Beyond 55

Chapter XII. Landing in Tegucigalpa 65

Chapter XIII. Un Coco 67

Index 71

Books in the *Traveling on the Edge* series

    Unusual Africa

    Unusual Asia

    Unusual Latin America (and Antarctica)

Preface

This book is a collection of essays, each one a true story. Each describes the exciting experiences we've had as we travel, experience, and learn. Although I've visited every country on the continental Western Hemisphere, I've selected only the most interesting stories for this compendium. The stories describe our adventures to Antigua & Barbuda, Argentina, Belize, Bolivia, Brazil, Colombia, Cuba, Dominica, Ecuador, Guyana, Honduras, Suriname, Uruguay, and Antarctica. I hope you enjoy hearing our stories as much as we enjoyed living them and enjoy talking about them.

I have an insatiable thirst for unusual travel. Let me explain what I mean by unusual travel. You are not likely to find me in a Parisian café drinking coffee and eating baguettes with melted brie (although I have done so). I don't enjoy such a comfortable trip. On the other hand, you are also not likely to find me ice climbing on glaciers in Greenland (I would love to visit Greenland, but certainly not to ice climb). I don't enjoy such a dangerous trip; nor do I have the physical stamina. I do enjoy travel that resides somewhere between these two extremes: like traveling on a 3-passenger klotok on the rivers of Kalimantan, sleeping on the deck; like exploring Antarctica on a 50-person research vessel; like spending a month living with little electricity in Jos, Nigeria; like renting a car and spending a few weeks driving around Southern Africa; or like spending a night with former headhunters. Those of you who love taking cruises on 3,000+ passenger liners will likely find my kind of travel too dangerous; after all, it *is* possible to get very sick, or even die, doing the things I do, but for my wife and me the rewards of meeting new people, learning new cultures, eating new cuisines, seeing animals that few westerners ever see far outweigh the perils. Those of you who love to rock climb the Pyrenees, explore underground rivers within caves, bungee jump from helicopters, skydive, or climb K2, will likely find our kind of travel downright mundane.

About the Author

Al Davis is an entrepreneur, business strategist, consultant, teacher, avid world traveler, author, and lifelong student, in no particular priority or chronological order.

As an entrepreneur, he has been a founder and/or executive in five startup companies, some resounding successes and some dismal failures. As a business consultant, he has assisted some of the largest corporations in the World and mentored many of the tiniest. As a teacher, he has lectured 2,000+ times and taught in 28 countries, with extended assignments in Australia, Indonesia, Nigeria, South Africa, Spain, and United States. He has visited 90 countries and slept on all seven continents; this latter feat completed on December 8, 2003 when he and his wife camped overnight on Antarctica. As an author, he has written 100+ articles in journals, conferences, and the press, as well as nine books. And although he considers learning from doing and observing far more significant educational accomplishments than degrees, he happens to have earned a PhD in computer science from the University of Illinois.

You can learn more details about the author at his website, www.a-davis.com.

Chapter I. Getting Shot in Bogotá

In 2015, I led a group of University of Colorado executive MBA students on a trip to Bogotá, Colombia as part of a course to understand the differences in business practices between US and Colombian companies. Specifically, we concentrated on the fashion and beer microbrewing industries. In the US, we spent time touring the factories of the Fashion Design Center of Denver, Colorado, and UpSlope Brewing Company of Boulder, Colorado, where we interviewed Lisa Ramfjord Elstun and Matt Cutter, founders of the two companies, respectively. In Bogotá, we visited Miguel Caballero Apparel and Bogotá Beer Company. This chapter focuses on Miguel Caballero.

Miguel Caballero Apparel was founded in 1992 by Miguel Caballero. His company manufactures and sells bulletproof and knife-proof high-fashion clothing. Unlike his competitors who use Kevlar® to make military-style clothing, Miguel uses his own patented materials to make clothing like dresses, gowns, men's suits, tuxedos, and so on. His customers include Michelle and Barack Obama, Hugo Chávez, and Michael Bloomberg. Our visit was hosted personally by Miguel and his wife, Carolina. We toured the entire facility including the factory floor, the warehouse (where we could inspect all the raw materials), the auditorium/modeling stage (where we could try on various garments), and the R&D lab (the only place we could not take photos). But the highlight of the visit was when Miguel asked for a volunteer to get shot. I was ready to volunteer if no students did, but Jason quickly raised his hand. All of us gathered around on the factory floor to watch. We were all fitted with ear protection. Assistants placed an MC sport jacket on Jason. Miguel unboxed and showed us all a highly polished revolver. He invited Jason to select a bullet from a box of bullets and Miguel placed the muzzle of the gun next to the jacket at point blank range, at just about Jason's liver. Three times Miguel stated very clearly, "I will count to three and then shoot. This is just a rehearsal. When I count 1, please breathe in and hold your breath. After I shoot, you may exhale. This is just a rehearsal. Are you ready? (pause; Jason nods) 1 (pause; Jason inhales) 2 (pause) 3 (pause) bang (Jason exhales)." After the three rehearsals, Miguel rang a bell. It was a signal to everybody on the factory floor to pay attention and be quiet. The quiet was palpable. Miguel asked, "Jason, are you ready?" and Jason said, "yes." Then, Miguel said, "I will count to three and then shoot. This is not a rehearsal. When I count 1, please breathe in and hold your breath. After

I shoot, you may exhale. This is not a rehearsal. Are you ready? (pause; Jason nods) 1 (pause; Jason inhales)." Then Miguel squeezed the trigger and shot Jason. Absent were 2 and 3; just 1 and then the shot. This is how Miguel does it to ensure that the "victim" is totally relaxed when shot. It worked. On the way back to the hotel in the bus, Jason showed off the large bruise on his belly, but he assured us that the experience was well worth the small sacrifice. Another student tweeted back to other students that "Jason has been shot," and the news spread quickly in Denver. A few minutes later another tweet calmed the anxious Coloradans with more accurate details. Read more about Miguel Caballero at www.miguelcaballero.com and in the New York Times at www.nytimes.com/2008/10/06/world/americas/06mexico.html. Here are three photos from our trip: (a) Miguel, Jason, and the crushed bullet, (b) the factory floor, and (c) the entire class with our hosts outside of Miguel Caballero.

While in Bogotá, we took an afternoon off to enjoy the local street art. The city government had seen street art (aka graffiti) as a problem (and a crime). In 2011, Diego Felipe Becerra, a 16-year-old street artist was shot in the back and killed by police while fleeing from a graffiti arrest. The ensuing police cover-up, and eventual exposure and mass protests resulted in a 40-year jail sentence for the policeman. Then, a few months later, Justin Bieber, with a full entourage of press and body guards left his own graffiti on a public street in Bogotá. These two events caused the city to rethink its approach. Now street art is officially prohibited but not considered illegal. Street art is thriving in the city. Here are just a few of the photos I took while on tour.

Chapter II. Car Manufacturing in Uruguay

Uruguay is a highly developed nation, with a prosperous economy, low crime rates, and highly-educated citizens. Uruguay was the first country in the World to fully implement One Laptop per Child (OLPC). Its capital is Montevideo, a friendly and beautiful city. It is the home of Carlos Ott, designer of the communications tower in Montevideo, which looks very similar to his Hotel Burj Al-Arab in Dubai.

Although Montevideo is not a haven for old cars like Cuba (see page 23), I was fascinated by this 1955 Hillman Husky Mark I. And although extreme poverty is either non-existent or much better hidden in Montevideo than in other major Latin American cities, I did find this family squatting near the Fortaleza del Cerro.

In November 2010, I visited Effa Motors (actually EdanTech dba Effa Motors), an automobile manufacturing facility. This company started out as a manufacturer of Christmas tree ornaments. Around 2006, Chinese car manufacturers including Lifan Industries decided to enter the Brazilian and Uruguayan markets. However, both countries limit car sales to those with major assembly and manufacturing in Argentina, Brazil, or Uruguay. EdanTech saw an opportunity. It acquired a software-based manufacturing process control company, and then proposed to assemble Lifan 320 and 520 automobiles in Uruguay. When I saw the Lifan 320's rolling out of the facility, I assumed they were Mini Coopers. I think it is safe to call them "knock offs". See photos below of the Lifan 320 (on left; and yes, that's me getting into the car) and the Mini (on right).

Meanwhile, the Lifan 520 appears to be a knock off of a Toyota Corolla, although inside the Lifan 520 is a 1991 Citroën ZX.

Anyway, with the help of the production software, Effa Motors is able to assemble 40 cars a day (20/shift) – all by hand at 14 consecutive workstations. All partially assembled vehicles move from station to station using motorized hand-driven dollies (see photo below) and forklifts. All parts arrive via ship from China in boxes, except the batteries which come from Brazil and the wheels which come from Argentina. On site are four Chinese Lifan employees who perform final quality inspections. The completed cars are sold in Uruguay and Brazil for around US$12,000, making them among the least expensive cars anywhere in the Americas. Effa Motors has plans to double its footprint, and start assembling additional Lifan models, including light trucks.

A new Brazilian law demands that all cars sold in Brazil must contain functionality that allows law enforcement personnel to stop any vehicle remotely. Effa plans to construct the software solution in their software division and integrate it into all Lifans. In general, they are looking for as many opportunities to add value as possible. By the way, most of the cars on the Uruguayan roads are new; and are dominated by Japanese, Korean, USA, and German brands. The Chinese brands are coming on strong. The highway from Montevideo to the Effa factory is lined with car dealerships, many of them carrying Chinese branded cars: Chery, FAW, Geely, Great Wall, and Lifan.

I find Uruguay one of the most fascinating countries in Latin America. It is second smallest country in South America (next to Suriname), but it:

- Is #1 in South America for literacy rate (according to the 2017 CIA World Factbook):

1.	Uruguay	98.5%
2.	Argentina	98.1%
3.	Chile	97.5%
4.	Peru	97.3%
5.	Venezuela	96.3%
6.	Bolivia	95.7%
7.	Ecuador	95.4%
8.	Colombia	94.7%
9.	Brazil	92.6%

- Is #1 in South America for percent of population with access to clean water (according to WHO/UNICEF's 2015 report):

1.	Uruguay	100%
2.	Argentina	99%
3.	Chile	99%
4.	Brazil	98%
5.	Venezuela	93%
6.	Colombia	91%
7.	Bolivia	90%
8.	Ecuador	87%
9.	Peru	87%

- Has the lowest corruption index in South America (global rank is shown out of 176 countries according to Transparency International in 2016; USA is ranked 18)

1.	Uruguay	21
2.	Chile	24
3.	Suriname	64
4.	Brazil	79
5.	Colombia	90
6.	Argentina	95
7.	Peru	101
8.	Bolivia	113
9.	Ecuador	120
10.	Venezuela	166

- Is one of three South American countries with murder rates lower than USA (along with Bolivia and Chile).
- Has a life expectancy that is the 2nd highest in South America (1st is Chile):

- Has the lowest income inequality in Latin America and the 2nd lowest in the Americas (1st is Canada)
- Has the 3rd highest GDP per capita in South America:

1.	Argentina	14.5
2.	Chile	14.3
3.	Uruguay	13.1
4.	Venezuela	12.2
5.	Brazil	10.5

- Has the 2nd best ranking in South America for freedom of the press (global rank is shown according to Reporters Without Borders 2017 report; USA is ranked 43)

1.	Suriname	20
2.	Uruguay	25
3.	Chile	33
4.	Argentina	50
5.	Guyana	60
6.	Peru	90
7.	Ecuador	105
8.	Bolivia	107
9.	Colombia	129

Chapter III. Two Hidden Gems of the Caribbean

When I think of the Caribbean, I think of cruise ships unloading 5,000+ passengers, pastel-painted stores all selling identical cheap souvenirs made in the Philippines, street vendors selling conch shells painted with "Having Fun in the Caribbean," and finally blaring Calypso music on every street. Obviously, I haven't been to every Caribbean island, but most that I have been to confirm my not-so-positive impressions. I also understand that not all travelers have the same tastes that I do, and that is a good thing, especially for most of the Caribbean.

I want to talk here about two Caribbean places I visited that provide something different, and they suit me perfectly: the island of Dominica, and Thatch Caye (off the coast of Belize).

Dominica is a small island roughly in the center of the Lesser Antilles, a chain of volcanic islands stretching from Puerto Rico south to Venezuela. Although I believe all the other islands have been stripped bare of their forests, Dominica is almost entirely covered by tropical rainforest, and most of it is protected. It boasts 365 rivers, is quite mountainous, has active volcanoes, and includes 300 miles of hiking trails on just 300 sq. mi. It is also home to the last remaining indigenous people of the Caribbean: the Kalinago. After Columbus landed in the Caribbean and for the next 300 years, Europeans systematically killed all the tribes they called the Caribs. The Kalinago of Dominica were able to survive only because of the rugged coast and extremely mountainous terrain. Today, about 2,200 Kalinago live on Dominica, most in a 3,700 acre area called the Kalinago Territory in the northeast corner of the island.

My wife, Ginny, and I spent 3 days on Dominica at the Roots Jungle Retreat, deep in the Northern Forest Reserve. It is owned by Argentineans Guadeloupe and Martin. Guadeloupe is the cook; Martin keeps everything at the lodge working. Our driver and guide was Morris, a Kalinago. Here is our Arawak cabin and Morris.

Getting to the lodge was an adventure by itself. Although just 6-7 miles from the main road, the "road" (if you can call it that) definitely requires a 4 wheel drive vehicle and an experienced driver. Martin has been pouring concrete in some areas that are prone to rutting from deep mud when it rains, but overall we appreciated Morris's skillful and careful driving. The cabin provided complete privacy for us. The windows were just open to the outside; no screens and no glass. We had plenty of ventilation and the mosquito netting over the bed kept us protected at night. But is reality we saw very few flying insects.

One day, Morris took us to the Kalinago Territory. Against all odds, many of the indigenous tribes in North America have been able to retain their native languages in spite of the fact that they have only been oral. Unfortunately, no traces of the original Kalinago language remain. In addition, very few full-blooded Kalinago remain due to the prevalence of intermarriages. The Territory allows people to settle within their borders as long as they can prove that they are part Kalinago. We asked Morris about religion; he said that ever since colonization and a heavy influx of European missionaries, all Kalinago are now Catholic. However, he added, "being a good person makes you a good person; religion does not make you a good person." I think that is one of the smartest comments I have ever heard concerning religion.

The second day, Morris took us to the south end of the island to snorkel. The snorkeling was fair; the coral was pretty much destroyed by people, but a nice variety of small colorful fish was still to be seen. Snorkeling on Champagne Reef was fun: volcanic action under the seabed caused millions of bubbles. We felt like we were swimming in a huge glass of champagne.

For more information about Roots, see www.rootsdominica.com. A recent hurricane had wiped out their small hydroelectric generator on the adjacent stream; as a result we had power just a few hours in the evening, but that's not a problem for us.

Dear Reader: By now you can figure out that we like remote lodges, not sprawling hotels full of people. And that is exactly what we got when we visited Thatch Caye Resort (thatchcayebelize.com) in Belize. To get there, we took a 15 minute ride on a Tropic Air Cessna 208B from Belize City to Dangriga. Thatch Caye personnel met us at the Dangriga airstrip for a 9 mile, 30 minute high-speed motorboat ride to a completely private 12 acre resort island with just 13 villas. We stayed at a villa on stilts over the Caribbean.

Ginny and I, our daughter and her husband were the only guests here. Lots of snorkeling, swimming, deep-sea fishing, and relaxing to be done. Food was first class, and the resort was all inclusive. And in case you were wondering, Thatch Caye has electricity, air conditioning, and Wi-Fi 24 hours a day.

Chapter IV. Broken Gem of the Caribbean

Barbuda seemed like the perfect vacation spot for Ginny and I. 62 sq. mi. and just 26 people per sq. mi.; and if you omit the village of Codrington, there're just 5 people per sq. mi. The island has just two small hotels and a half-dozen small guest houses, and miles and miles of pink beaches. That's it! Who could ask for anything more for a quiet vacation?

We booked ourselves for 4 nights at the North Beach Cottages, on the north side of the island, with a huge beach, incredibly nice and private. The entire facility has 6 guest cabins on stilts, right on the beach, plus a dining cabin. Here is our cabin.

We spent our days walking on the beach, snorkeling, and eating. The snorkeling was acceptable: nothing fantastic, but a pretty nice reef with colorful fish was accessible around 300' from shore. The food was excellent, thanks to world class Spanish chef Sira, who owns the Sun of a Beach restaurant in Codrington.

I will not pretend to understand the differences of opinion between management and employees at North Beach, nor will I assign blame, but many of the employees quit 2 weeks before our arrival. After the mass employee exodus, the owner named Ruben, who lives in New York City, called me and asked if everything about my stay was arranged. I explained that I had not heard back from them after sending my deposit. I had no information about transportation they were arranging for us from Antigua to Barbuda or from Barbuda to Antigua. Ruben told me about the resignations, apologized, and quickly made the transportation reservations for us. Although Ruben arranged to have his son present during our stay, the son appeared to remain totally uninvolved. We had been told that housekeeping would occur 3 times/week, but the housekeeper did little except straighten the sheets on the bed and empty our trash can onto the beach each day.

One of the highlights of our visit was a tour of the frigate bird sanctuary just a few minutes by boat from the cottages. Here we could see hundreds of immature frigates on nests while their moms hovered above. We saw no adult males. We also learned that although the primary food for frigate birds is fish swimming near the surface that they scoop from the ocean, the birds cannot swim. And in fact, a frigate bird that accidentally lands on (or crashes into) the water is doomed unless it can get itself to shore to dry out.

Our stay at North Beach Cottages was a mixed experience. The cabins were excellent. The privacy was terrific. The food, thanks to Sira, was first-rate. The tension among the staff was palpable, and made for an uncomfortable overall experience. But the worst part of our experience was the fact that the people in the Barbuda tourism industry just did not act like they cared. Let me explain.

Only four ways exist to get to Barbuda: SVG Air, Barbuda Express, charter a private plane, or private yacht (or cruise ship).

Barbuda

Ruben had made advanced reservations for us with SVG Air to fly from Antigua to Barbuda. SVG advised us to arrive one hour before departure time. When we arrived at 615am nobody was at the check-in counter. Soon afterwards, another party arrived and got in line behind us. We compared tickets. Ours had a 715am scheduled departure time; theirs had an 815am scheduled departure – same flight number. Very strange, but even stranger when we observed that the flight departures screen listed the flight with a scheduled departure time of 930am. I walked over to the airport information desk to see if they could verify we were at the correct check-in counter; they told me that SVG personnel usually arrive at around 8am. Strange given that my tickets said the "normal" departure time was 715am. We waited. The ticketing agent actually arrived at 815am and checked us all in. He issued us boarding cards that read "boarding at 645am; departure at 715am." And the plane actually departed at 915am – two hours late (or 15 minutes early if you believe the departures screen), No explanation was ever given. Interestingly, we were escorted by the ticketing agent out to the tarmac where we waited. The aircraft came to us to pick us up ☺.

For the return from Barbuda to Antigua, we had asked Ruben to book us on the Barbuda Express ferry scheduled to depart at 4pm. We arrived at the dock at 230pm. At 345pm they announced a delay to 430pm with no explanation. At 435pm, we overheard the ferry captain making a private cell phone call to an unknown party; he was speaking in Creole but we were able to ascertain a few phrases: ". . . you asked us to wait 30 minutes . . . now 435pm . . . where are you? . . . ok . . . on your way? . . . ok . . . be here in 5 minutes? . . . ok! . . . we wait for you." Then he tells all of us waiting passengers, "5 more minutes." Now we all know the reason for the original delay: we're waiting for somebody who is either important or knows somebody important or paid off somebody important. But he or she is even later that originally estimated. During the next 25 minutes, many of the passengers complained quite loudly to the crew, and all the crew responded with was, "call this number and talk with the manager." One passenger said, "Today is my birthday. I have reservations in St. John's and I'm going to miss it." Finally *at 5pm*, a van pulled up to the dock and 4 drunks (a 40-year old male and three 20 something year old females) emerged and walked toward the ferry. They were holding open beer bottles and were laughing; they seemed amused that they had delayed the ferry. The awaiting passengers were not happy with either the crew or the four drunks. We departed at 515pm, 75 minutes late.

Bottom line: I strongly recommend against using SVG Air or Barbuda Express. I do not know if the employees of these two companies don't care or if their management does not care. Or perhaps they care but are simply incompetent. I do not plan to ever return to Barbuda due to my perception that people who work in the tourism industry don't care about tourists. Perhaps if you charter a private plane or yacht, you might have better luck. Stay at North Beach Cottages, but *only* if (a) they have hired Sira as a chef (we sensed that they did not treat her particularly well so I doubt she will work there again), and (b) management learns how to motivate its employees.

Chapter V. The Cuban View of Cuba

During the short period of time between President Obama's relaxation of restrictions for Americans traveling to Cuba and President Trump's reversal, my wife and I spent 5 days in Cuba. During this time, we heard a detailed history of Cuba-American relations from a Cuban Army Lt. Col. (ret). I want to capture his perspective of this history here because it differs considerably from the narrative that I have understood from my education in the United States. I want to present it here without prejudice and without judgment. I have no basis to declare it any more or less accurate than the story I have been told by my teachers and the U.S. media.

Cuba's first attempt at independence resulted in the unsuccessful Ten Years' War (from 1868-1878). A second war, fought from 1879-1880, was similarly unsuccessful.

The third attempt at independence (1895-1898) was successful in part due to the intervention of the United States. In 1901, as a result of the United States' aid to Cuba in effecting its independence from Spain, Cuba agreed to become a major trading partner with the US and allowed US companies to develop its arable land. During the next 60 years, US agricultural companies (e.g., Cargill, Dole, and Monsanto) expanded to own 75% of the arable land of Cuba, and employed most of the Cuban farmers, treating them like slaves and paying them almost nothing. Meanwhile, a series of leaders led Cuba who were little more than puppets to the US Government.

In 1959, Fidel Castro led a revolution to take back Cuba for the Cuban people. His goal was to give the land back to the Cuban people (and away from the US companies) and replace dictator (and American puppet) Fulgencio Batista. Castro, and his colleague, Che Guevara, saw America in general, and American businesses specifically, as having taken advantage of the Cuban people for almost 60 years. Castro and Guevara wanted US out of Cuba, period.

According to my Cuban army source, the US Government saw Cuba as "the only Latin American country that stood up to them." Kennedy's Bay of Pigs invasion was an attempt to get Cuba back under American control.

I remember the Cuban Missile Crisis very well as a 13-year old boy. I saw it clearly as Cuba and Soviet Union aggression. However, the Cuban perspective is quite different. Ever since the revolution, Cuba was convinced that US was going to invade it. Cuba went to Russia to secure some protection. It wanted those missiles to protect itself from the anticipated invasion of American troops. During President Reagan's term of office, Castro was absolutely convinced an invasion was imminent . . . once again as a punishment for the revolution . . . and to bring back the US agricultural companies to retake the land. He initiated a nationwide campaign to train every able-bodied citizen to fight against the invading army.

I want to close with just a few comments about our visit to Cuba. We stayed mostly at casas particulares (what we would call B and B's). As a result, we met a lot of Cubans. We stayed 2 nights in Playa Larga, 1 night in San Diego de los Baños, and 2 nights in Havana. We did some great birding in both parks; my favorite birds were the Cuban pygmy owl, the bee hummingbird (smallest bird in the world), the Cuban trogon, and my all-time favorite the Cuban tody. Wherever we went, we found the Cuban people friendly, accommodating, helpful, and honest.

I would be remiss as an American male if I did not talk a bit about vehicles on the road throughout Cuba. Regardless of urban or rural, I found about 10% of vehicles were 1950's vintage American cars, 10% were horse-drawn wagons, 15% were Russian-made cars (Ladas and Moskviches) from the 70's and 80's, and the remainder were relatively new (10 years old or newer) vehicles imported from South Korea (Kia, Hyundai) and China (BYD, Geely). Surprisingly few cars from Europe or Japan seem to be on the road. Although I took dozens of photos of old American cars, I will not bore you with them; here's one of a 1952 Pontiac; however I must admit that although the side molding is that of a 1952, the front grille is that of a 1951, so who knows what year it really is? And finally, I was quite surprised to see a horse-drawn wagon in a gas station on the road between Playa Larga and Havana. I didn't know that horses needed gasoline, but I guess the tires do need air.

Chapter VI. The Amazon Headwaters, Ecuador

After a half-hour plane ride east out of Quito to Coca, and a two-hour (50-mile) ride down the Napo River, the driver pulled our motorized dugout canoe onto a remote beach.

We thought we would finally be at Sacha Lodge. But that was not the case. The driver told us to exit the boat and start walking. We walked for about a half mile along a boardwalk and came to a small clearing with dugout canoes.

The Amazon

Lodge employees finally paddled us across a blackwater lagoon to the very remote Sacha Lodge. We half expected a parking lot full of cars behind the lodge, but no, this was the real thing. We were really 3 hours from the nearest civilization.

Sacha Lodge consists of 26 cabins all elevated on posts and interconnected with each other and the main building on elevated walkways.

The Amazon

The cabins are all screened in and include an indoor bathroom and shower. The water for the shower is pumped directly from the lagoon, so it is cold and cloudy, but it sure feels great when you are hot and sweaty.

Every morning, afternoon, and evening, we were able to select from a long menu of activities, including hikes, climbs to a jungle canopy platform for bird watching, canoe trips, caiman-spotting, and so on. We never had a dull moment during our four days, except when we were tired and needed a rest. Then we napped in hammocks outside our cabin listening to jungle sounds.

We had a pair of guides who worked together: Simipedro, who was a local Quechua Indian who spoke Quechua and Spanish, and David, a California native who spoke English and Spanish. As we traveled around together, Simipedro would tell us (in Spanish) about medicinal plants and local myths as well as stories about local animals. Then David would translate them into English. It worked well.

One day, while we were resting, Simipedro came running up to our cabin yelling to get our attention. The three of us came out to find his hands full of a viper he had captured.

David always had a bandage the size of a large Band-Aid on his calf. We asked him about it and he told us that he had been bitten by some kind of insect. We asked him how he was treating it and he said he was washing it carefully twice a day. On our last day, as we were ready to depart, David's leg was heavily bandaged, so we asked him what had happened. He told us, "last night I went to clean my leg. I looked at the wound and it was looking back at me." It turns out that he had not been *bitten* by an insect after all. In contrast, a bot fly had *laid an egg* in his calf and it had been gestating in his leg, living off his muscle tissue. Simipedro had come to his rescue last night and placed a piece of red meat on his leg. The bot fly larva, seeking the most nutritious source of food emerged from David's leg and entered the meat. Then they cleaned out the hole in his leg and bandaged it up.

For more information about Sacha, see www.sachalodge.com.

Chapter VII. Searching for Jaguars in Bolivia

We've seen lots of large carnivores in the wild, but not jaguars. Three nights in Kaa Iya National Park in southern Bolivia was the perfect solution. This remote park is the largest national park (13,000 sq mi) in all of South America and home to the largest concentration of jaguars in the world (estimated to have a population of around 1,000). We signed up with Nick's Tours (www.nicksadventuresbolivia.com); Nick McPhee picked us up at the Sun Hotel in Santa Cruz. Before we continue with my jaguar story, let me digress. The trip from the Santa Cruz airport to the Sun Hotel the night before was an adventure all by itself . . . .

The Sun Hotel advertised "free airport shuttle service," so we were pleased when we were met at arrivals by a man holding a sign with our names. He took us to a beat up car that was at least 20 years old; I think it was a Russian-made Lada, or perhaps a Spanish Seat. After loading all our baggage and ourselves, he tried to start the car. No luck. He lifted the driver's seat and played with some wires, replaced the seat and started the car. We drove out of the airport and onto the exit ramp of the divided highway. Yes, the exit ramp going the wrong way onto the highway. At the top of the ramp, he stayed on the shoulder facing oncoming traffic until he reached the next exit. There he exited on the entrance ramp to go onto another divided highway going the wrong way. Then he made a quick left turn into the hotel's exit gate. Oh, I forgot to mention that twice during this route the car stopped, he had to get out of the car, fidget with the wires under his seat and restart the car. The desk manager explained to us that a log truck had rolled over in front of the hotel's entrance gate, forcing the driver to take this circuitous route. Oh really?

Nick drove a perfectly equipped 4wd Mitsubishi Delica. Three and a half hours south of Santa Cruz we came to the locked gates of Kaa Iya, where we picked up our indigenous guide. That's Nick in the photo below unlocking the gate.

The entire park is also a Guaraní-Izoceño indigenous reservation[1] and regulations demand that an indigenous guide accompany every tour into the park. In theory this is a great idea, and I hope that the guide learned something while on the trip; however, he added nada to our experience and occupied a potential revenue seat in Nick's vehicle. In the town of San Jose, Nick purchased bags of coca leaves. A wad of these leaves were perpetually in Nick's and the guide's cheeks for the remainder of the trip. I dipped a couple of times as well, but never "got the point."

Nick set up camera traps throughout the park. These are triggered to photograph whenever an animal comes near. He showed us many dozens of photos of unwary tapirs and jaguars. For the next two nights, we slept at a ranger's station in a spare bedroom and ate meals prepared by the "guide." The accommodations and board were minimal but more than acceptable given that we were in the middle of absolutely nowhere and about to see the elusive jaguar. It goes without saying that no other tourists were to be found here. This trip is for the truly adventurous.

---

[1] Kaa Iya is also home to another indigenous tribe, the nomadic Ayoreode hunter-gatherers, who are totally untouched by the West. Let's hope they can stay that way. History does not bode well.

Jaguars

That evening we set out at around 430pm for our daily dusk search for jaguars. Three hours, no sightings. At 8pm, we returned to the ranger station for dinner and night's sleep. We awoke at 430am for an early morning ride in hopes of catching jaguars before they turned in from their nightly hunts. We returned for 8am breakfast without a sighting. After breakfast, it was another ride, but since most jaguars sleep during the day, we were in search of birds and other mammals. We spotted a tapir, a 12' boa constrictor crossing the road, quite a few interesting birds, including these caracaras: the Northern and the yellow-headed.

We also learned about the Gran Chaco forest. This is the second largest forest on the planet. Unlike the largest (the Amazon rainforest), this one is dry, receiving just 20" of rain a year. We also observed that many of the roads we traveled on throughout the park followed the path of an above-ground pipeline; we learned that it is owned by Gas TransBoliviano and pumps natural gas 1,900 miles across Bolivia and Paraguay. It was never clear to us whose gas was being pumped, but our suspicion is that it is Brazilian natural gas being pumped to the Pacific Ocean, for loading onto tankers for shipment to China. We also learned that Che Guevara was killed in La Higuera, a small village just 60 miles further south of Kaa Iya.

We returned for lunch and a well-deserved nap. At 430pm, we headed out again in search of jaguars. Once again, nothing. 8pm, we returned for dinner, and decided to go out for a late night drive to see if we could catch sight of a large cat. All we saw were hundreds of nightjars flying off the road as we approached (this photo may look pretty dark to you, but this is exactly what a nightjar looks like at night ☺). No luck and we turned in around 2am.

Jaguars

After a few hours of sleep, we woke up early and repeated the previous day's schedule. It was exhausting, and still no jaguar sightings. Over dinner (8pm-9pm), we discussed plans for that night. Our flight the next day was 150pm. Working backwards from there: we needed to be at the airport three hours earlier for an international flight, i.e., 1050am. It was a 3.5 hour ride from Kaa Iya to the Santa Cruz airport, which meant we needed to leave the park no later than 7am. Nick suggested that we take a nap after dinner for a few hours and then depart the ranger station around 2am. That way we could look for jaguars around the park for 5 hours before heading for Santa Cruz. We had a plan!

We got to bed around 11pm and slept for 2 hours. During the next 5 hours, we searched ceaselessly for jaguars all over the park, to no avail. No jaguars wanted to be seen on this expedition. We ate breakfast in the car and slept on the way back to Santa Cruz.

Chapter VIII. Plantation Owners of Suriname

We traveled to Suriname because . . . honestly . . . because we wanted to visit every country in South America. It really was not on our bucket list, but we were quite pleasantly surprised by the adventure it brought us.

The adventure started when we arrived in the morning at the Santa Cruz, Bolivia airport three hours before our flights to Suriname were to depart. I had found quite reasonably priced tickets from to Paramaribo, Suriname. They were not the most convenient, requiring plane changes in Sao Paulo and Belem, Brazil, as well as an overnight in Cayenne, French Guinea, but they were half the price of any other routing, but we were on vacation and had plenty of time. When we tried to check in at GOL Airlines, the ticketing agent asked for our Brazilian visas. I explained we were not staying in Brazil; we were just in transit to our next destination. She explained that would be acceptable if we were flying through just one Brazilian airport arriving and departing on international flights, but the flight from Sao Paulo to Belem was a domestic flight and we needed a visa. Ouch! It made total sense once she explained it, but I had missed this "minor" fact completely when planning the trip. In short, she would not let us board.

The Santa Cruz airport is not large. One small café. One travel agent. A few airlines. We were able to get on Wi-Fi and discovered a flight leaving that evening on COPA from Santa Cruz to Panama, connecting to another COPA flight arriving around 2am in Paramaribo. Great news. It would cost us a lot of money, but at least we could get to Paramaribo in time to catch our noon flight inland the following day.

During this time at the airport, while trying to figure out how we were going to get ourselves to Suriname, we decided to grab a bite to eat at the one and only café. I ordered a small savory roll (the British call it a "pie"); Ginny ordered something else to eat as well as a chocolate shake. I broke a tooth in half on the pie; it plagued me for the rest of the trip. And Ginny developed food poisoning from the shake, from which she suffered mightily for the next 7 days.

Meanwhile, the COPA desk personnel informed us that they could not issue any tickets at the airport! The travel agent informed us that they could accept only cash (no credit cards) at the airport. And we were talking about a non-trivial amount of money for these tickets (>$3,000). Our only recourse was to drive to downtown Santa Cruz and purchase the new tickets from a travel agent. Nick and his wife let us rest for an hour or so at their office and then drove us to the airport in time to make our new flights. Thank you, Nick!

We arrived at the Paramaribo airport in the wee hours of the morning. I do not recall who helped us find an accommodation for the few hours that night, but it was in what we would call a backpackers' hostel. A caretaker met our taxi at the entrance to hand us a key and then said good night. Three flights up; no elevator. Four hours of sleep (after sleeping in a car the night before).

The next morning we took this GUM Airways plane from the domestic Zorg en Hoop Airport in Paramaribo 150 miles to the Kabalebo Airstrip for 3 nights at the Kabalebo Nature Resort in the remote rainforest of Central Suriname. One of the first things the local guide did was to take us to see a plane that crashed in 1965 at the Kabalebo Airstrip (see photo below). I'm glad we saw this *after* our flight.

Plantations

Our stay at Kabalebo was terrific with lots of hikes, canoe trips on the river, many new bird sightings, and this great poison dart frog who met us on one trail.

Most of the resort is situated at one end of the dirt runway (don't worry about the noise; there is just one plane a day) but we stayed in a very private cabin at the far other end of the runway. The staff shuttled us back and forth to our cabin in a golf cart; not bad! Here is our cabin, with the "runway" in the foreground.

The highlight of our trip to Suriname, however, occurred upon our return to Paramaribo where we were treated to an experiential history of the Jews of Suriname, led by Marina da Costa, a descendent of 17th century Jewish immigrants to the country. As we walked the streets of the now abandoned city of Jodensavanne (aka "Jewish savannah"), we learned from Marina how her ancestors arrived on the northern shores of South America during the first half of the 17th century to escape persecution in Europe (Marina's family came from Portugal). The British colonial government offered the settlers complete freedom of religion.

The Jews established sugar plantations, had their own justice system, their own schools, and built their first synagogue as early as 1670. In short, they operated almost as an independent Jewish State within the colony of Suriname. A second synagogue was built in 1685; using today's terminology, one was orthodox and one was conservative. By the end of the 17th century, 400 sugar plantations existed in Suriname (now a Dutch colony, after England traded Suriname to the Netherlands in return for New Amsterdam, aka New York City), and thousands of slaves worked on them. Around 30% of these plantations were owned by Jews.

From 1690 to 1722, a series of slave revolts occurred, targeting all slave owners including Jews. At the same time, the price of sugar cane declined making it less profitable to raise sugar cane. Slowly, the plantation industry disappeared and most Jews migrated out of Jodensavanne to Paramaribo to undertake other trades. In 1832, the synagogue and most of Jodensavanne burned to the ground, and since then the forest has been taking over what was once a thriving city. Here is part of the cemetery.

Here is one of many graves of Marina's ancestors, this one dated 1734.

Here is what is left of the second synagogue, as well as the "new" synagogue in Paramaribo.

Chapter IX. Iguazú

Can you tell what this is?

I have this photo enlarged and displayed in my home. Some visitors think it is a snake; some say an ostrich. It turns out it is a rear view of a female lesser potoo sitting on her nest. The nest contains a single egg and has been built at the end of a broken vertical tree limb. See her now? The lesser potoo is related to the nightjar and frogmouth and is a master of disguise. She will rarely, if ever, leave her nest while incubating her egg. To eat, she simply opens her foul-smelling mouth and waits for an unwary insect to enter thinking that something died therein. Then she closes her mouth and swallows. Dine in delivery. You can see a side view of this same bird on page 45.

We were staying three nights at Yacutinga Lodge (yacutinga.com), on the Iguazú River in Argentina, just 10 miles east of Iguazú Falls. It was paradise for us, as (*non*-fanatical) hikers, birdwatchers, and jungle-lovers. We The food in the restaurant was superb, and walking around the grounds surrounded by butterflies, woodpeckers and hummingbirds was delightful. Here is our cabin.

We spent two days at Iguazú Falls. If you are going to visit just one waterfall in your lifetime, this is the one. From the Argentinian side (we spent two nights at the Sheraton Hotel on the Argentinian side, with a distant view of the falls), one can walk along metal catwalks constructed along the very top edges of the falls. Look east and you see the river coming toward you; look west and you look out over the great expanse of Brazil. Look straight down and watch 450,000 cu. ft. of water per second tumbling down at your feet. This is about 4.5 times the volume of Niagara Falls. The roar and the vibration are unreal.

And here is a photo of the Inferno.

Along the way, you can see Devil's Throat, where the water cascades from three directions into a hole and swallows dart all over catching insects – check out the two dozen brave swallows in the photo below.

We took a bus tour to the Brazilian side (don't forget your visa!); from here, you can walk for 2-3 hours on a trail along the base of the falls. I know of no other place in the world where the water falls perpendicular to the direction of the river, thus enabling you to walk the length of the falls at its base. A boardwalk has also been constructed to enable you to walk out from the trail into Devil's Throat – well worth it.

Iguazú

And while I'm describing "must do" things: you must take the boat ride from the Brazilian side into the falls. The boat actually goes under the falls, thoroughly soaking everybody. A blast!

Chapter X. Meeting a Monkey-Muncher

We were staying at the Rewa Eco-Lodge (www.rewaguyana.com) on the Rewa River right in the geographic center of Guyana. The voyage there from civilization had been somewhat harrowing (I'll tell you more about it later), but once we arrived, it was clearly well worth it. The lodge is immediately adjacent to a small Amerindian village of 300 residents, and it is the villagers who built it. Every aspect of the lodge's operations is performed by members of the village, and those who work there share in the profits. The villagers are Makushi.

The Rewa village and lodge is 28 miles upriver from its nearest neighboring village, Genip. One does not just stumble accidentally upon Rewa; one finds it only by trying. The lodge consists of six huts, each with private bathroom and outside shower. I don't recall if the huts had electricity; I think not, but this is not a big issue when doing this kind of travel. Food was excellent, prepared by villagers from locally sourced meat, plants, spices, and so on, and served in a community hut. Here is our hut:

We spent the 1st day learning about the village, taking canoe tours on the river looking for monkeys and birds, and taking short 1-3 mile hikes. The only means of transport used by the villagers is the dugout canoe, which they build by hand out of purpleheart using a hand axe.

A few of the 70 or so huts in the village had solar panels, large enough to power a light bulb for the children to do their homework in the evening. Here are some of my favorite photos from our canoe trips and hikes around Rewa. The first is a pair of sunbitterns; the guide told us they are a rare sight, but it is always difficult to know if this is true or if we are being told this to add to our excitement. In any case, sunbitterns have spectacular plumage when they spread their wings. The next is an iguana sunbathing above the river. And the third is a fruit of a bush we encountered during a hike; I've shown this photo to many botanists over the past few years and none have been able to identify it. It is an aggregate fruit which might be related to a sugar apple (*Annona squamosal*) shown in the photo to the right of it.

We also spent some time with the lodge manager understanding business problems he was having. It turns out that he was keeping track of scheduling of tourist visits using a whiteboard and markers. Our son, Mike, taught him how to use PC-based scheduling software during our visit. And that tells me that the lodge must have had electricity! The manager also shared with us that around 20% of the visitors "give back" to the lodge in terms of advice (as we did) or donations or in-kind support.

On the second day at Rewa, the three of us (Ginny, Mike and I) decided to take a 4-mile hike to view the nest of a harpy eagle. Harpy eagles weigh 20 lbs., have 7' wingspans and dine on adult monkeys. These are the largest and strongest raptors in the Western Hemisphere. We dressed in our usual hiking gear and were ready for rigorous hike. Two barefoot villagers accompanied us, and carried extra drinking water for us; they did not need water for themselves because they were happy drinking directly from the river or swamp. One villager set the pace; Ginny and Mike kept up with him, but I was more interested in going slow and steady because we were walking through lots of muddy patches that made it difficult to lift my feet. Meanwhile, during the first 2 hours, I fell no less than 5 times, each time landing face down in the mud, unable to stop myself from falling because all the trees were covered with huge spikes and I preferred to be bruised and filthy rather than skewered. Fortunately, the second villager stayed with me. Unbeknownst to me, the rest of the party was stopping regularly in a vain hope that I would catch up to them. Finally, after 2 hours, Ginny hiked back to us and said they couldn't keep stopping anymore; they needed to head for the nest and get back to camp before nightfall. With that news, I attempted to hike for another 30 minutes or so, but I was so exhausted from repeatedly falling that I finally gave up. "My" villager hiked back to camp with me. I was out for around 5 hours and never saw the harpy. Fortunately, Ginny and Mike made it to the nest and back. Here is a photo they took.

So, let's talk about the circuitous route we took to get to Rewa. We started by flying to Georgetown, the capital of Guyana, famous to Americans as the site of the Jonestown Massacre of Jim Jones' cult followers. The main Georgetown airport handles only international flights, so the first challenge is to get from this airport to the domestic airport called Ogle, 45 minutes away. From Ogle airport, we took a two-hour flight on a small commuter aircraft operated by Trans Guyana Airlines to Lethem, a small village on the border with Brazil in the South of Guyana. From there, we took a 55-mile, 3-hour car ride to Karanambu Lodge, which is normally accessible by car, but was newly isolated as an island due to heavy rains. I'll talk about our wonderful stay at Karanambu Lodge below. After 3 days at this lodge, we departed by boat for an 18-mile, 2-hour canoe ride to Genip (remember Genip?) where we were delivered to the Makushi Tribe for the final 28-mile, 3-hour canoe ride to Rewa. When people hear about our trips, they often ask who we use as a travel agent. The fact is no travel agent could possibly arrange such a trip. The logistics took dozens of hours of planning, and many phone calls and emails with locals to make sure that roads were passable, rivers were navigable, and people dropping us off (by car or boat) in places had contact information for people who were picking us up at those places, and so on. In this particular case, almost everything went just as planned, but that isn't always the case, e.g., when Karanambu's site was transformed into an island. And when things don't go as planned, you need to maintain your sense of adventure, ingenuity, and humor, and hope your hosts do the same.

We spent three nights at Karanambu Lodge, home of the "Otter Lady," aka Diane McTurk. Diane was 80 at the time, but was as agile and strong as anybody half her age. She was born at Karanambu and had spent most of her life here dedicated to the conservation of the habitat of the endangered giant river otter. She traveled with us every day in dugout canoes searching for otters, birds, and other wildlife. We never saw any of her beloved otters; she told us that she had recently released some of her orphaned otters and due to recent heavy rains all the otter families had moved upstream. Here is a photo of Diane. We thoroughly savored every moment we had with her.

And here is our cabin at Karanambu.

Diane McTurk passed away in December 2016, at the age of 85. Her ashes were spread over the ponds surrounding Karanambu.

Chapter XI. Drake Passage and Beyond

At least once a year, Ginny and I sit down and compare each of our "top 5 travel destinations." Every time we do this, Antarctica appears on both of our lists. In fact, Antarctica has been #1 on both of our lists since we visited in 2003. Although you've heard the expression, "you had to be there" before, I will try to describe some aspects of our adventure here, even though it is almost impossible to describe.

Ginny, our son Michael, and I boarded the Academik Ioffe[2] in Ushuaia, Argentina en route home from spending three months in South Africa. Getting to Ushuaia from Cape Town was non-trivial; it required three flights: a 10-hour flight on Malaysia Air from Cape Town to Buenos Aires, a 3-hour flight from BA to Rio Gallejos, and a 1-hour flight from Rio Gallejos to Ushuaia. We were exhausted, but when we saw Ushuaia, it was all worth it! What a beautiful town and backdrop.

---

[2] On some websites, this ship is called the Peregrine Mariner or the Marine Adventurer. I suspect the reason is to not scare away some tourists who could be afraid to be on board a Russian ship. However, anybody who gets on can easily read the name of the ship on its bow.

Our ship (АКАДЕМИК ИОФФЕ in Cyrillic) was in the harbor getting provisioned for our upcoming voyage.

The Ioffe is a 383' Russian research vessel with a maximum speed of 14.5 knots. It has a maximum capacity of 100 passengers (it carried 50 on our trip) and carries a crew of 65. Ginny and I had one cabin and we shared a bath with Mike who was in an adjoining cabin. The ship features an internal 450 ton water-ballasted stabilizer system that keeps it amazing stable, even in heavy seas. We were told during the briefing that the stabilization system is necessary so the ship can do research on Arctic and Antarctic Ocean seabeds from a geo-stable surface platform; however, from our passenger perspective, stability contributed greatly to our comfort. The ship also has bow and stern thrusters, which I had never seen before. The captain showed how he could use these to reposition either end of the ship to the port of starboard; at one point during the trip, he even demonstrated how he could use the bow thruster to redirect an iceberg that was meandering slowly toward the ship while we were at anchor.

Ginny and I are not fans of the typical "cruise scene." But this was ideal. The meals were all served buffet style and we all dressed casually. Ah yes!

For the first 3 days, we cruised across Drake Passage. The crew said it was unusually calm, and in fact called it Drake Lake. However,

Antarctica 57

Mike and I were the only passengers aboard who ventured out on deck; we had to hold on tight, especially when climbing the ladders to the highest deck, or we would have been blown overboard. The waves were crashing over the top of the ship. Here is Mike on the highest deck. Not for the faint of heart, the weak-armed, or weak-legged.

On the third day, we saw our first iceberg. How grand! It was 10 times larger than our ship; one end looked like a cathedral.

For the next 5 days, we slipped in and out of passages of the Antarctic Peninsula, viewing an ever changing panorama of vistas, and making landfall around twice a day. Here is the entry to Lamaire Channel; it reminds me of a scene ideal for a jigsaw puzzle.

Here is an iceberg I snapped near Pleneau Island, two blue-eyed cormorants and one of thousands of Gentoo penguins I saw nearby.

One highlight of the voyage was the opportunity to camp out overnight on the mainland of Antarctica. About 30 of the 50 passengers participated. We were each given a bivy sack and sleeping bag; no tent. We were shuttled to land in the usual zodiacs around 10pm, and instructed on how to clear away the top layer of snow before laying out our sleeping materials. Here is what our sleeping area looked like.

I was wearing around 6 layers of clothing. I shed the outer 3 layers when I turned in, and laid them beside my sleeping bag (you can see one of those layers in yellow in the above photo). That was actually a mistake because during the night when I needed to use the toilet, these garments were frozen solid and I could not put them back on. Instead, I should have shoved them inside my sleeping bag with me. We were told that if we become cold or wanted to return to the ship anytime during the night, all we had to do was awaken the crewmember who was sleeping in a tent near us; he would be happy to motor us back to the ship in the zodiac. Because the sun was up all night, you could wake up at any time and feel like it was morning and that you had slept all night. Mike actually returned to the ship around 4am; Ginny and I slept until around 8am. It wasn't a bad night's sleep.

We spent much time with Gentoo, Adelie, and chinstrap penguins, the latter being my favorite by far. On one occasion, Ginny and I went

Antarctica

for a hike and left Mike at the shore. When we returned, he was lying down on the snow with three chinstraps standing on him looking at him askance. Here are three photos of chinstrap penguins. The first is one of dozens I took showing the community of penguins as they interacted noisily and boisterously. The second shows a chinstrap incubating an egg on a nest; no external signs distinguish male from female and they share the parenting responsibilities; as a result, I do not know if this is the mother or father. The third shows a very proud chinstrap; he seems unaware that another chinstrap had defecated on his chest. All three were taken at Paradise Harbor.

Antarctica

Finally, here is my favorite wildlife photo from Antarctica, a female elephant seal that posed angrily for me on Aitcho Island.

Chapter XII. Landing in Tegucigalpa

We had been told that Tegucigalpa had the shortest and most dangerous approach of any commercial runway of any airport in the World, and our landing on COPA flight #426 did not disappoint.

The runway at Toncontín International Airport is just a bit over 6,000'. To understand how short this is: a fully loaded B-757 needs 6,500'; a B-767 needs 8,900'; a B-747 needs 10,000'. The largest plane approved for Toncontín is a B-737. We were landing in an Embraer 190, which needs 4,500' to land and 6,500' (if fully loaded) to take off. Hopefully, they did not have a full load when they departed.

But what makes landing here so tricky is not just the short runway. A large mountain stands right where the final approach would be for a normal airport. In fact, mountains surround the airport on all sides. Here is my impression of how we made our approach:

We approached Tegucigalpa from the north and dropped down through a small valley over the north side of the city. A few miles past the airport, the pilot turned left 540 degrees (that's 1.5 times around) as we lost altitude in a tight spiral, avoiding all the surrounding mountains. On our final approach, we were just a few hundred feet above a residential neighborhood, and still in a significant roll, before leveling out just before touchdown. The internet has many videos of landings at this Honduran airport. Check them out! I thought it was fun. I suspect that some passengers find it terrifying.

From Tegucigalpa, we flew on a small Saab 340 to the Caribbean island of Roatan for three nights. We stayed at Upachaya Eco-Lodge. Now, we've stayed at quite a few eco-lodges during our travels, and we have to admit that although Susan is a very nice hostess, the only attribute that qualifies Upachaya to be called eco anything is the fact that Susan recycles. That's it.

Upachaya is basically a three-story motel that serves breakfast and provides snorkeling excursions for both motel guests and cruise ship passengers who have docked at Roatan. Susan arranges for locals to guide snorkelers out to nearby reefs on her pontoon boat; the snorkeling was terrific.

The biggest problem with Upachaya is the meals. A very nice hot breakfast is served to order. Lunch is limited to a salad, but only on days when cruise ship passengers are on site; otherwise you are on your own. We asked our hostess what we should do about dinners since the nearest restaurant or grocery store was 5 miles away. Her answer was, "well, I guess I could call you a taxi." The rooms have a small refrigerator but no microwave or stove, so on our first day we went into town and stocked up on bread, cheese, peanut butter, and jelly; and that sustained us for lunches and dinners for the remainder of our stay. Not every country has to be a culinary delight, but it would have been nice to know ahead of time that meals were going to be a challenge.

Chapter XIII. Un Coco

Our shy 13 year old son, Mike, did not know a word of Portuguese. Yet there we were sitting around the Othon Palace Hotel pool in Salvador, Brazil, and he had swam over to the in-pool bar and ordered himself a fresh coconut. He was nonchalantly drinking coconut juice out of his straw as we all looked on in amazement. 16 year old Marsha swam over to him and asked, "How did you do that?" He responded, "I was thirsty, so I asked for 'un coco' hoping to get a Coca Cola.[3] But this is even better!" So Marsha said "un coco" to the bartender and we had two very pleased and proud children.

I had first visited the magical city of Salvador, capital of Bahia, three years before and had been enthralled by the people, the architecture, the music, the culture, the history, and the food. Being in Salvador is a totally immersive experience and I was so thrilled to have the opportunity to return to share the experience with my whole family. Let me share a bit of Salvador with you.

The city is built on two levels, separated by a sheer 300' cliff. The old city is located on the upper level and the architecture is colorful to say the least. Every few blocks, one encounters a group of boys playing

---

[3] Of course, in Portuguese, a coconut would be *um coco* and a Coke would be uma *coca*, but that did not matter.

music and doing capoeira. The music is enticing and the "dancing" amazing. It is impossible to not stop and watch; be sure to tip them!

Children are in the streets everywhere giving you ribbon bracelets from the Church of Nosso Senhor do Bonfim. If you let them tie one on your wrist (and you should), you should also give them a small amount of money as a thank you. When I departed Bahia, I sported a half-dozen or so such ribbons. The story goes that if you deliberately remove one or more of these ribbons from your wrist, bad luck will follow you for all your days. On the other hand (pun intended), if you allow them to fall off naturally, your wishes will come true.

Salvador

It is impossible and never fair to describe an entire population with the broad stroke implied by any set of adjectives. However, I must say that after visiting so many places in the world, I found many of the friendliest and most beautiful people in Salvador. Every person in the street smiles at you, whether you are a neighbor or a complete stranger. I recall my first visit to Bahia. I was a passenger in my friend's (Antonio Bastos) car driving along the beach. As we drove, I saw two people walking hand-in-hand on the sidewalk away from us. They were both wearing the tiniest of bikini bottoms. I could not tell their genders, but I could tell that both had incredibly well-shaped bodies with almond-colored skin. When we passed, I looked back and discovered that one was clearly a man and one was clearly a woman, but it was of no consequence. Regardless of gender, they were beautiful people.

Salvador was founded in 1549 (60 years before Jamestown -- the first settlement in United States) as a slave port. 38% of all Africans shipped to the Americas during the 300 years of American slavery were shipped to Brazil. Although Bahia has a sordid history as the port of entry for most of the forced labor supporting the sugar industry of Brazil, the citizens of Bahia today celebrate their rich and diverse cultural heritage from Africa, Europe, and the Indigenous peoples of Brazil.

The food in Salvador is unique; at least I have not tasted anything like it anywhere else in my travels. My favorite is moqueca, a stew of seafood, palm oil, coconut milk, tomatoes, onions, and spices (particularly garlic!). Restaurants typically serve moqueca de camarão (shrimp) and various kinds of moqueca de peixe (fish). My wife gets an upset stomach (we think it is from the palm oil), but I love the taste of moqueca.

Index

Academik Ioffe, 55–57
Adelie penguin, Antarctica, 60
Aitcho Island, Antarctica, 63
Amerindians
  Ayoreode Tribe, 30
  Bolivia, 30
  Caribs, 13
  Dominica, 13, 15
  Ecuador, 27
  Guaraní Tribe, 30
  Guyana, 47, 51
  Izoceño Tribe, 30
  Kalinago People, 13, 15
  Makushi Tribe, 47, 51
  Quechua, 27
Antarctica, 55–62
  Adelie penguin, 60
  Aitcho Island, 63
  blue-eyed cormorant, 58–59
  chinstrap penguin, 60–63
  Drake Passage, 56–57
  elephant seal, 63
  Gentoo penguin, 58–59, 60
  icebergs, 57–59
  Lamaire Channel, 58
  Paradise Harbor, 61–62
  Peninsula, 58–59
  Pleneau Island, 58–59
Antigua and Barbuda
  Barbuda, 17–20
  Codrington, 17
  food, 17
  North Beach Cottages, 17–18
  snorkeling, 17
Argentina, 41–44
  Buenos Aires, 55
  butterflies, 42
  clean water, 10
  corruption, 10
  food, 41
  freedom of the press, 11
  GDP per capita, 11
  Iguazú Falls, 41–44
  lesser potoo, 41, 45
  literacy rate, 10
  Rio Gallejos, 55
  swallows, 44
  transportation, 8
  Ushuaia, 55–56
  Yacutinga Lodge, 41–42
Ayoreode Tribe, 30
Bahia, Brazil, 67–69
  architecture, 67–68
  capoeira, 68
  food, 69
  history, 69
  Othon Palace Hotel, 67
  people, 69
Barbuda, 17–20
  airport, 19
  Codrington, 17
  ferry, 19
  frigate birds, 18
  North Beach Cottages, 17–18
  Sun of a Beach restaurant, 17
  SVG Air, 19
  transportation, 18–20
Barbuda Express, 19
Bastos, A., 69

Batista, F., 21
Becerra, D., 3
bee hummingbird, Cuba, 22
beer industry, 1
Belize
    Dangriga, 15
    snorkeling, 16
    Thatch Caye Resort, 13, 15–16
Bieber, J., 3
Bloomberg, M., 1
blue-eyed cormorant, Antarctica, 58–59
boa constrictor
    Bolivia, 31
Bogotá Beer Company, 1
Bogotá, Colombia, 1–5
Bolivia, 25–33
    Ayoreode Tribe, 30
    boa constrictor, 31
    clean water, 10
    coca, 30
    corruption, 10
    food, 35
    freedom of the press, 11
    gas pipeline, 32
    Gran Chaco, 32
    Guaraní Tribe, 30
    Izoceño Tribe, 30
    jaguars, 25–33
    Kaa Iya National Park, 25–33
    La Higuera, 32
    literacy rate, 10
    murder rate, 10
    Nick's Adventure Tours, 25–33
    nightjar, 32–33
    Northern caracara, 31
    San Jose, 30
    Santa Cruz, 29, 33, 35–36
    Sun Hotel, 29
    tapir, 30, 31
    transportation, 29
    yellow-headed caracara, 31, 32
bot fly
    Ecuador, 27
Boulder, Colorado
    UpSlope Brewing Company, 1
Brazil, 44–45, 67–69
    architecture, 67–68
    capoeira, 68
    clean water, 10
    coconut, 67
    corruption, 10
    food, 69
    gas pipeline, 32
    GDP per capita, 11
    Iguazú Falls, 44–45
    literacy rate, 10
    people, 69
    Salvador, 67–69
    Sao Paulo, 35
    slavery, 69
    sugar industry, 69
    transportation, 8, 9
Britain, 38
Buenos Aires, Argentina, 55
BYD, 23
Caballero, C., 1
Caballero, M., 1–3
caiman
    Ecuador, 27
Canada
    income inequality, 11
Cape Town, South Africa, 55
Caribbean, 13–16
    forests, 13
Castro, F., 21–22
Cayenne, French Guinea, 35
cemetery
    Suriname, 39

Index

Champagne Reef, Dominica, 15
Chávez, H., 1
Chile
  clean water, 10
  corruption, 10
  freedom of the press, 11
  GDP per capita, 11
  life expectancy, 10
  literacy rate, 10
  murder rate, 10
China
  gas pipeline, 32
  Lifan Industries, 7–9
chinstrap penguin, Antarctica, 60–63
CIA World Factbook
  literacy rate, 10
Citroën ZX, 8
coca
  Bolivia, 30
Coca, Ecuador, 25
Codrington, Barbuda, 17
Colombia
  beer industry, 1
  Bogotá, 1–5
  Bogotá Beer Company, 1
  clean water, 10
  corruption, 10
  fashion industry, 1–3
  freedom of the press, 11
  grafitti, 3–5
  literacy rate, 10
  Miguel Caballero Apparel, 1–3
Cuba, 21–24
  bee hummingbird, 22
  cars, 23–24
  Cuban Missile Crisis, 22
  Havana, 22
  history, 21–22
  horse-drawn wagons, 23–24
  Playa Larga, 22
  pygmy owl, 22
  San Diego de los Baños, 22
  tody, 22
  trogon, 22
Cutter, M., 1
da Costa, M., 38–40
Dangriga, Belize, 15
Denver, Colorado
  Fashion Design Center, 1
Dominica, 13–15
  Champagne Reef, 15
  Kalinago, 13, 15
  Northern Forest Reserve, 13
  religion, 15
  Roots Jungle Retreat, 13–15
  snorkeling, 15
Drake Passage, Antarctica, 56–57
Dubai
  Hotel Burj Al-Arab, 7
dugout canoe
  Ecuador, 25–26
  Guyana, 48
DuPont Corporation, 1
Ecuador, 25–27
  bot fly, 27
  caiman, 27
  clean water, 10
  Coca, 25
  corruption, 10
  dugout canoe, 25–26
  freedom of the press, 11
  literacy rate, 10
  Napo River, 25
  Quito, 25
  Sacha Lodge, 25–27
  viper, 27
EdanTech, 7–9
Effa Motors, 7–9
elephant seal
  Antarctica, 63

Elstun, L., 1
Fashion Design Center, Denver, 1
fashion industry, 1–3
food
　Antigua and Barbuda, 17
　Argentina, 41
　Bolivia, 35
　Brazil, 69
　food poisoning, 35
　Guyana, 47
　Honduras, 66
French Guinea
　Cayenne, 35
frigate birds
　Barbuda, 18
Geely, 9, 23
Genip, Guyana, 47, 51
Gentoo penguin, Antarctica, 58–59, 60
Georgetown, Guyana, 51
giant river otter, 52
graffiti
　Bogotá, Colombia, 3–5
Gran Chaco, Bolivia, 32
Guaraní Tribe, 30
Guevara, C., 21, 32
GUM Airways, 36
Guyana, 47–53
　Diane McTurk, 52–53
　dugout canoe, 48
　food, 47
　freedom of the press, 11
　Genip, 47, 51
　Georgetown, 51
　giant river otter, 52
　harpy eagle, 50–51
　iguana, 48, 49
　Karanambu Lodge, 51, 52–53
　Lethem, 51
　Ogle Airport, 51
　purpleheart wood, 48
　Rewa, 47–52
　sunbittern, 48–49
　Trans Guyana Airlines, 51
harpy eagle
　Guyana, 50–51
Havana, Cuba, 22
Hillman Husky
　Uruguay, 7
Honduras, 65–66
　airport, 65
　food, 66
　Roatan, 65–66
　snorkeling, 65
　Tegucigalpa, 65–66
　Toncontín International Airport, 65
　Upachaya Eco-Lodge, 65–66
Hotel Burj Al-Arab, Dubai, 7
icebergs, 57–59
iguana, 48, 49
Iguazú Falls, 41–45
　Argentina, 41–44
　Brazil, 44–45
　Devil's Throat, 44–45
　The Inferno, 43
Izoceño Tribe, 30
jaguars
　Bolivia, 25–33
Jamestown, Virginia, 69
Jews
　Suriname, 38–40
Jodensavanne, Suriname, 38–40
Kaa Iya National Park, Bolivia, 25–33
Kabalebo Nature Resort, Suriname, 36–38
Kalinago, Dominica, 13, 15
Karanambu Lodge, Guyana, 51, 52–53

Index

Kennedy, J., 21
Kevlar, 1
La Higuera, Bolivia, 32
Lada, 23, 29
Lamaire Channel, Antarctica, 58
Lesser Antilles, 13
lesser potoo, 41, 45
Lethem, Guyana, 51
Lifan Industries
   Model 320, 8
   Model 520, 8
   Uruguay, 7–9
Makushi Tribe, 47, 51
Malaysia Air, 55
Marine Adventurer, 55
McPhee, N., 25–33
McTurk, D., 52–53
Miguel Caballero Apparel, Bogota, 1–3
Mini Cooper, 8
Mitsubishi Delica, 29
Montevideo, Uruguay, 7–9
moqueca, 69
Moskvich, 23
Napo River, Ecuador, 25
Netherlands, 38
New York City, 38
New York Times, 2
Niagara Falls, 43
Nick's Adventure Tours, Bolivia, 25–33
nightjar
   Bolivia, 32–33
North Beach Cottages, Barbuda, 17–18
Northern caracara
   Bolivia, 31
Northern Forest Reserve, Dominica, 13
Obama, B., 1, 21
Obama, M., 1

Ogle Airport, Guyana, 51
One Laptop per Child
   Uruguay, 7
Othon Palace Hotel, Bahia, Brazil, 67
Ott, C., 7
Panama, 35
Paradise Harbor, Antarctica, 61–62
Paraguay
   gas pipeline, 32
Paramaribo, Suriname, 35–36, 38–39
Peregrine Mariner, 55
Peru
   clean water, 10
   corruption, 10
   freedom of the press, 11
   literacy rate, 10
plantations
   Suriname, 38–39
Playa Larga, Cuba, 22
Pleneau Island, Antarctica, 58–59
poison dart frog
   Suriname, 37
Pontiac, 23
Portugal, 38
potoo, 41, 45
Puerto Rico, 13
purpleheart tree, 48
pygmy owl, Cuba, 22
Quechua Tribe, 27
Quito, Ecuador, 25
Reagan, R., 22
religion
   Dominica, 15
Reporters Without Borders, 11
Rewa, Guyana, 47–52
Rio Gallejos, Argentina, 55
Roatan, Honduras, 65–66

Roots Jungle Retreat, Dominica, 13–15
Sacha Lodge, Ecuador, 25–27
Salvador, Brazil, 67–69
San Diego de los Baños, Cuba, 22
San Jose, Bolivia, 30
Santa Cruz, Bolivia, 29, 33, 35–36
Sao Paulo, Brazil, 35
Seat, 29
slavery
   Brazil, 69
   Suriname, 38
snorkeling
   Antigua and Barbuda, 17
   Belize, 16
   Dominica, 15
   Honduras, 65
South Africa
   Cape Town, 55
Sun Hotel, Bolivia, 29
Sun of a Beach restaurant
   Barbuda, 17
sunbittern, 48–49
Suriname, 35–40
   cemetery, 39
   corruption, 10
   freedom of the press, 11
   history, 38–40
   Jews, 38–40
   Jodensavanne, 38–40
   Kabalebo Nature Resort, 36–38
   Paramaribo, 35–36, 38–39
   plantations, 38–39
   poison dart frog, 37
   slavery, 38
   synagogue, 38, 39, 40
   Zorg en Hoop Airport, 36
SVG Air
   Barbuda, 19

swallows
   Argentina, 44
synagogue
   Suriname, 38, 39, 40
tapir
   Bolivia, 30, 31
Tegucigalpa, Honduras, 65–66
   airport, 65
Thatch Caye Resort, Belize, 13, 15–16
tody, Cuba, 22
Toncontín International Airport, Honduras, 65
Toyota Corolla, 8
Trans Guyana Airlines, 51
Transparency International, 10
transportation
   Argentina, 8
   Barbuda, 18–20
   Bolivia, 29
   Brazil, 8, 9
   Cuba, 23–24
   Uruguay, 7–9
trogon, Cuba, 22
Tropic Air, 15
Trump, D., 21
UNICEF
   clean water, 10
United States
   corruption, 10
   freedom of the press, 11
University of Colorado, 1
Upachaya Eco-Lodge, Honduras, 65–66
UpSlope Brewing Company, Boulder, 1
Uruguay, 7–11
   clean water, 10
   corruption, 10
   EdanTech, 7–9
   Effa Motors, 7–9
   freedom of the press, 11

Index

GDP per capita, 11
Hillman Husky, 7
income inequality, 11
Lifan Industries, 7–9
life expectancy, 10
literacy rate, 10
Montevideo, 7–9
murder rate, 10
One Laptop per Child, 7
transportation, 7–9
Ushuaia, Argentina, 55–56
Venezuela, 13

clean water, 10
corruption, 10
GDP per capita, 11
literacy rate, 10
viper
   Ecuador, 27
World Health Organization
   clean water, 10
Yacutinga Lodge, Argentina, 41–42
yellow-headed caracara
   Bolivia, 31, 32

www.ingramcontent.com/pod-product-compliance
Lightning Source LLC
Chambersburg PA
CBHW042338150426
43195CB00001B/32